If slavery is not wrong,

nothing is wrong.

I cannot remember when

I did not so think, and feel so.

Abe's Hon

THE LIFE OF

est Words

Abraham Lincoln

★ ★ ★

by Doreen Rappaport *Illustrated by* Kadir Nelson

HYPERION BOOKS FOR CHILDREN/NEW YORK

AN IMPRINT OF DISNEY BOOK GROUP

To Howard Schuman, in celebration of words, laughter, and friendship
—D.R.

For my baby boy, Ali
—K.N.

ACKNOWLEDGMENTS

I thank the students in Deb Barry's enrichment class, Maple Shade Elementary School, East Longmeadow, Massachusetts, who gave honest and insightful critiques of my manuscript. I thank Carol Briggs of the Roeliff Jansen Community Library, Hillsdale, New York, for her constant support in ensuring my receiving important research sources.

The quotations in bold are Abraham Lincoln's own words. Some quotes have been edited and punctuation changed for readability, without changing the meaning of Lincoln's original intention.

First Edition
1 3 5 7 9 10 8 6 4 2

Printed in Singapore
This book is set in ITC Fenice.

Reinforced binding
Library of Congress Cataloging-in-Publication Data on file.

ISBN 978-1-4231-0408-7

Visit www.hyperionbooksforchildren.com

AUTHOR'S NOTE

I first became acquainted with Abraham Lincoln when I was about five years old. My friends and I collected copper pennies, the shinier, the better. In first grade, Lincoln came into my life again when I learned that all Americans celebrated his birthday. I liked the idea of a day off from school and was too young to understand why this president was so important that his birthday was an official holiday. When I was in the fifth grade, we had to memorize the Gettysburg Address. I can still repeat large parts of it by heart. Legend says that Lincoln wrote this speech on the back of an envelope on the train, but like all of Lincoln's speeches, the Gettysburg Address was edited and re-edited until this ten-sentence, 268-word speech was a model of elegant, precise writing. On the battlefield at Gettysburg, he prophesied that "The world will little note, nor long remember what we say here. . . ." How wrong he was.

In researching this book, I read and reread Lincoln's letters, newspaper interviews, and innumerable speeches. His eloquence and simplicity of words were ever present, and so was his concern for the nation during and after the great tragedy of the Civil War. His writing is a model for all of us, and so is his compassion. In this book, I share with you some of those words that touched me deeply and reveal his character.

—D.R.

ILLUSTRATOR'S NOTE

I'd always known that Abraham Lincoln was an important historical figure, but it wasn't until I read his biography that I fully appreciated why. Lincoln had been placed so high on our historical pedestal that most of us forget that he was a real person who had very modest beginnings. It was only through his sheer will, his intelligence, and perseverance that he was able to achieve so much as president.

As part of my research for the artwork, I traveled to Springfield, Illinois, to see firsthand where Lincoln lived and came into his own before he became president. Camera in hand, I visited New Salem, a replica of a village just outside of Springfield, where Lincoln lived for a short while after he left home. I walked through Lincoln's Springfield home, the Old State Capitol where Lincoln gave his famous "House Divided" speech, and his old law offices. I found wonderful references at the Abraham Lincoln Presidential Museum and Library there, as well as in Washington, D.C., where I toured the U.S. Capitol building and spent time at the Lincoln Memorial. I did all of this to get a clearer picture of Lincoln's journey and found the experience to be invaluable and inspiring. I hope readers will be as impressed as I am with Lincoln's life and words, and like Mr. Lincoln, become inspired to meet their full potential.

—K.N.

In the slave state of Kentucky,
deep in the wilderness,
young Abraham learned
to hunt for nuts and currants
and fish for trout and bass
and tend to soil and seed.

He learned sorrow at age nine
when his mama died.
But he found great joy
with a loving stepmother,
who encouraged him to read and learn.

Abraham Lincoln is my name,
and with my pen I wrote the same.
I wrote in both haste and speed
and left it here for fools to read.

The family moved
deeper into the wilderness,
to the free state of Indiana.
Panther screams
and prowling bears
filled Abraham's nights with fear.

He had just a mite of schooling,
yet he loved words the way his papa,
a master storyteller, did.
He stuffed books inside his shirt.
In between splitting wood and plowing,
he stood in the field and read.
He read some books so many times,
he knew whole parts by heart.

The things I want to know
are in books;
my best friend is the man
who'll git me a book I ain't read.

Another move, to New Salem,
a village in Illinois.
The long, lanky boy was a man now.
He ferried people and goods
down the Ohio and Mississippi rivers.

In between the pull of the pole
and the splash of the water,
he listened to hunters spin tall tales
of a mighty marksman,
"half man, half alligator,"
and sailors describe giant mosquitoes
that could kill a man.

He heard lawyers tell how they used words
to gain justice for ordinary folks.
He heard preachers quote from the Bible:
"A house divided against itself
cannot stand."

He stored these different voices in his heart
and wove them into his own words.

The long, muddy Mississippi River
brought Lincoln south to New Orleans.

He walked on cobblestone paths
and along canals,
past flowers spilling over lacy iron balconies.
He saw men and women in fancy clothes,
eating fancy foods and sipping wine.
French, Spanish, and English words
filled his ears.
But a hideous sight shattered his joy.

Twelve Negroes,
chained six and six together.
Strung together
like so many fish upon a trotline,
being separated forever
from their childhood, their friends,
their fathers and mothers,
and brothers and sisters,
from their wives and children,
into perpetual slavery.

Lincoln worked at many jobs—
farmhand, store owner,
postmaster, surveyor,
rail-splitter.

Wherever, whatever,
he always had a book in hand.
Elocution, grammar, mathematics,
biography, history, poetry, plays.

Upon the subject of education,
I view it
as the most important subject
which we as a people
can be engaged in.

America was growing.
Farmers needed
new waterways and railroads
to ship their crops.
Everyone needed better education.
If he became a lawmaker,
he could help people get these things,
so he ran for the Illinois state legislature.

He spoke in public squares
and country stores and hayfields.

*I am young and unknown
to many of you.
I was born and have ever remained
in the most humble walks of life.
I have no wealthy or popular
relations to recommend me.*

He lost the election.
But people liked what he said
and how he said it.

He ran again.
This time he won.
He ran three more times and won.

He became a lawyer.
His clients praised "'Honest Old Abe,'
the lawyer who was never known to lie."
He didn't like the nickname Abe,
but it stuck.

Resolve to be honest at all events
and if you cannot be
an honest lawyer,
resolve to be honest
without being a lawyer.
Choose some other occupation.

Nearly four million black men,
women, and children
were enslaved in southern states.
Lincoln thought slavery a great evil.
If he became a United States senator,
more people would hear him
speak out against it.

In speech after speech,
he reminded people that
slavery did not fit with the ideals
of the Declaration of Independence.

*As a nation, we began to declare
that "all men are created equal."
We now practically read it
"all men are created equal,
except Negroes."*

He lost the election.
But again, his words got much attention.
People felt he spoke from his heart.

In the next two years,
tension over slavery grew
between the South and North.
Lincoln ran for president and
spoke out against this evil practice.
He won this election.

But a month before he took office,
seven southern states left the Union.
They formed their own government
with their own president.
In his first inaugural address,
Lincoln reminded Americans that
they were *one* people.

*We are not enemies, but friends.
We must not be enemies.*

On April 12, 1861, Southern troops
attacked Fort Sumter,
a federal fort in South Carolina.
Lincoln knew he had no choice now.
The North had to fight the South
to bring it back into the Union.

*I hold that the Union
of these states is perpetual.
No state can lawfully
get out of the Union.*

Families were torn apart,
as husbands, fathers, and sons
went off to war,
many never to return.

Many Northerners worried that Lincoln
did not have the skills
to lead the nation in this terrible time:

"He's too backwoods."
"He's unpresidential."
"He tells too many silly jokes."
"He's had too little experience in government."

If I were to try to read,
much less answer,
all the attacks made on me,
this shop might as well be closed
for any other business.
I do the very best I know how—
the very best I can; and
I mean to keep doing so
until the end.

Lincoln believed that true liberty
could not permit slavery.
He decided to use his wartime powers
as commander in chief
to end slavery.

In the third year of the war,
he issued the Emancipation Proclamation.
It freed over three million
black men, women, and children
and called for black men to join
the Union army.

In giving freedom to the slave,
we assure freedom to the free.

Most white Northerners opposed
Lincoln's proclamation.
But he stood firm.

*I never, in my life,
felt more certain
that I was doing right,
than I do in signing this paper.
My whole soul is in it.*

The war dragged on.
Lincoln grew sadder and sadder
as more Americans died.

He went to the Gettysburg battlefield
and again reminded the nation
why these men had sacrificed their lives.

Four score and seven years ago
our fathers brought forth
on this continent, a new nation,
conceived in liberty,
and dedicated to the proposition
that all men are created equal.

The Emancipation Proclamation
had freed slaves only in the states
and territories that were in rebellion.
Lincoln wanted slavery ended
in the entire nation.

Most white lawmakers did not want this.
He called them to the White House
to convince them
of what he knew was right.

*The moment came when I felt
that slavery must die
that the nation might live!*

Finally, they agreed.

In the fourth year of the war,
victory seemed close for the North.
But Lincoln felt no joy.
Hundreds of thousands of men
on both sides had died in battle.
The country was deeply divided.
Many Northerners wanted to punish
the South for starting the war.
Southerners were furious that
the Union army had destroyed
their cities and homes and crops.
Could the nation ever be one people
again?

In his second inaugural address,
Lincoln shared his vision
of how the country could heal itself.

With malice toward none;
with charity for all;
with firmness in the right,
as God gives us to see the right,
let us strive on
to finish the work we are in;
to bind up the nation's wounds.

The South finally surrendered.
The job of healing the nation began.
But Lincoln was not there to help.
An assassin's bullet ended his life.

But his words were there
to guide those who chose to remember.

It is for us the living, rather
that we here highly resolve
that these dead
shall not have died in vain—
that this nation, under God,
shall have a new birth of freedom—
and that government of the people,
by the people,
for the people,
shall not perish from the earth.

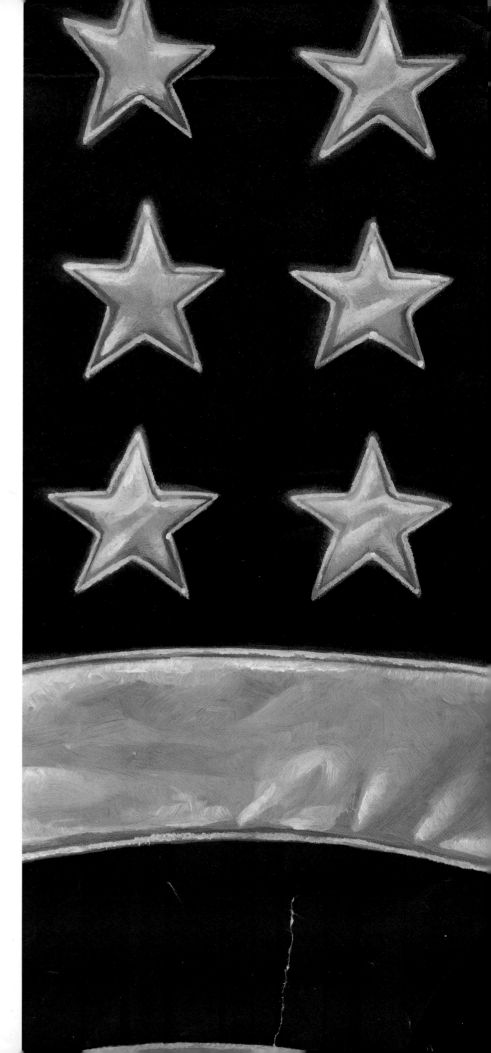

IMPORTANT DATES

February 12, 1809: Abraham Lincoln is born at Sinking Spring Farm, about three miles from Hodgenville, Kentucky.

1816: The family moves to Perry County, Indiana (now Spencer County).

1818: Lincoln's mother, Nancy Hanks Lincoln, dies of milk sickness.

December 2, 1819: His father marries Sarah Bush Johnston.

1827: The family moves to New Salem, Illinois. Lincoln works on a flatboat.

1832: Lincoln runs for the Illinois state legislature and loses. He becomes postmaster, then buys a store, which fails.

1834–1842: He serves four terms in the Illinois State Legislature and studies to be a lawyer.

November 4, 1842: Lincoln and Mary Todd are married.

August 1, 1843: The Lincolns' first son, Robert Todd Lincoln, is born.

March 10, 1846: Edward Baker Lincoln is born.

1846: Lincoln is elected to the U.S. House of Representatives from the seventh district in Illinois.

February 1, 1850: His son Edward dies of pulmonary tuberculosis.

December 21, 1850: William Wallace Lincoln (Willie) is born.

April 4, 1853: A fourth son, Thomas, is born.

1854: Lincoln is re-elected to the Illinois state legislature, but soon resigns to run for a U.S. Senate seat, which he doesn't attain.

1856: He helps found the Republican Party in Illinois, which adopts an antislavery platform.

June 16, 1858: Lincoln gives his "A House Divided" speech at the Republican Party's state convention in Springfield, Illinois, upon accepting the nomination for U.S. Senate. He loses to Stephen Douglas.

December 20, 1860–February 1861: Seven southern states secede from the Union.

March 4, 1861: Lincoln is inaugurated as the sixteenth president.

April 12–13, 1861: The Civil War begins when the Confederates attack Fort Sumter.

February 20, 1862: Lincoln's son Willie dies of typhoid fever.

January 1, 1863: Lincoln issues the Emancipation Proclamation.

November 19, 1863: He delivers the Gettysburg Address.

April 8, 1864: The U.S. Senate passes the Thirteenth Amendment formally abolishing slavery.

November 8, 1864: Lincoln is re-elected.

January 31, 1865: The U.S. House of Representatives passes the Thirteenth Amendment.

March 4, 1865: Lincoln gives his second inaugural address.

April 9, 1865: Confederate general Robert E. Lee surrenders to Union general Ulysses S. Grant.

April 14, 1865: Lincoln is shot by an assassin and dies the next morning.

May 4, 1865: Lincoln is buried at Oak Ridge Cemetery outside Springfield, Illinois.

IF YOU WANT TO LEARN MORE ABOUT LINCOLN, READ:

Bial, Raymond, *Where Lincoln Walked.* New York: Walker Books for Young Readers, 1997.

Cohn, Amy, *Abraham Lincoln.* New York: Scholastic Press, 2002.

Freedman, Russell. *Lincoln: A Photobiography.* New York: Clarion Books, 1987

Harness, Cheryl. *Young Abe Lincoln: The Frontier Days, 1809–1837.* Washington, D.C.: National Geographic Society, 1996.

Holzer, Harold. *Abraham Lincoln, the Writer: A Treasury of His Greatest Speeches and Letters.* Honesdale, Pennsylvania: Boyds Mills Press, 2000.

Meltzer, Milton. *Lincoln: In His Own Words.* New York: Harcourt, 1993.

Ruffin, Frances, and Philips, Ellen Blue. *Abraham Lincoln: From Pioneer to President.* Sterling Publishing Company, 2007.

Turner, Ann. *Abe Lincoln Remembers.* New York: Harper Collins, 2001.

Winters, Kay. *Abe Lincoln: The Boy Who Loved Books.* New York: Simon & Schuster, 2003.

WEB SITES

Illinois Historical Preservation Agency Lincoln sites *http://www.nps.gov/archive/liho/link3.htm*

Abraham Lincoln Presidential Library *http://www.alplm.org*

Lincoln Memorial *http://www.nps.gov/linc*

Abraham Lincoln Birthplace National Historical Site *http://www.nps.gov/abli*

SELECTED RESEARCH SOURCES

Ambrose, Stephen. *To America: Personal Reflections of an Historian.* New York: Simon & Schuster, 2002.

Donald, David Herbert. *Lincoln.* New York: Simon and Schuster, 1995.

Fehrenbacher, Don Edward. *Lincoln in Text and Context: Collected Essays.* Stanford, California: Stanford University Press, 1987.

Gienapp, William. *This Fiery Trial: The Speeches and Writings of Abraham Lincoln.* New York: Oxford University Press, 2002.

Goodwin, Doris Kearns. *Team of Rivals: The Political Genius of Abraham Lincoln.* New York: Simon & Schuster, 2005.

Holzer, Harold. *Lincoln at Cooper Union: The Speech That Made Abraham Lincoln President.* New York: Simon & Schuster, 2004.

McPherson, James M. *Abraham Lincoln and the Second American Revolution.* New York: Oxford University Press, 1991.

——. *The Illustrated Battle Cry of Freedom: The Civil War Era.* New York: Oxford University Press, 2003

Oates, Stephen B. *Abraham Lincoln: The Man Behind the Myths.* New York: Harper & Row, 1984.

——. *With Malice Toward None: The Life of Abraham Lincoln.* New York: Harper & Row, 1977.

Sandburg, Carl. *Abraham Lincoln: The Prairie Years (Volumes I and II).* New York: Harcourt Brace & Company, 1926.

Wills, Gary. *Lincoln at Gettysburg: The Words That Remade America.* New York: Touchstone, 1992.

THE GETTYSBURG ADDRESS

Four score and seven years ago our fathers brought forth on this continent, a new nation, conceived in liberty, and dedicated to the proposition that all men are created equal.

Now we are engaged in a great civil war, testing whether that nation, or any nation so conceived and so dedicated, can long endure. We are met on a great battlefield of that war. We have come to dedicate a portion of that field, as a final resting place for those who here gave their lives, that that nation might live. It is altogether fitting and proper that we should do this.

But, in a larger sense, we cannot dedicate—we cannot consecrate—we cannot hallow—this ground. The brave men, living and dead, who struggled here, have consecrated it, far above our poor power to add or detract. The world will little note, nor long remember what we say here, but it can never forget what they did here. It is for us the living, rather, to be dedicated here to the unfinished work which they who fought here have thus far so nobly advanced. It is rather for us to be here dedicated to the great task remaining before us—that from these honored dead we take increased devotion to that cause for which they gave the last full measure of devotion—that we here highly resolve that these dead shall not have died in vain—that this nation, under God, shall have a new birth of freedom—and that government of the people, by the people, for the people, shall not perish from the earth.

Gettysburg, Pennsylvania
November 19, 1863

A house divided against itself cannot stand. I believe this government cannot endure permanently half-slave and half-free.